J. H Scourfield

Lyrics, and Philippics

J. H Scourfield

Lyrics, and Philippics

ISBN/EAN: 9783744775786

Printed in Europe, USA, Canada, Australia, Japan

Cover: Foto ©Thomas Meinert / pixelio.de

More available books at **www.hansebooks.com**

LYRICS,

AND

PHILIPPICS,

BY

J. H. P.

ORIGINALLY PRINTED

AT MIDDLE-HILL PRESS, 1859,

BY JAMES ROGERS.

———

REPRINTED BY G. NORMAN, MAIDEN LANE, COVENT GARDEN.

1864.

LYRICS.

THE GOOD OLD ENGLISH LADY.

I WILL sing you an Old Song, which I've either heard or read,
Of a good Old English Lady, but if it should be said,
That I have ever met with one, like her, alive or dead,
The story is as false as is the Hair upon the Head
Of this Good Old English Lady, of no particular Time.

She once possessed a Heart of somewhat penetrable Stuff,
And cast at Youthful Gentlemen soft tender looks enough,
But since their feelings(not of course herself,)are grown so tough
She takes a very serious Turn, and quantities of Snuff,
Like a Good Old English Lady, of no particular Time.

She says the World is growing very wicked—and begins
To think that every one, except Herself, is full of sins,
Then sits up half the night at Cards, and most devoutly grins
A smile of pious gratitude to Heaven—if she wins,
Like a Good Old English Lady, of no particular Time.

She often makes comparison, with self-complacent Praise
Of what she was, to what Girls are, in these degenerate days,
And vows that she is horror-struck whenever she surveys
Their Waltzes, Polkas, Gallopades, and naughty flirting ways,
Like a Good Old English Lady, of no particular Time.

824053

The Church of Mr. Snuffleton on Sunday she attends,
Who says, that nearly all the world are going to shocking ends,
To whose denunications a willing Ear she lends,
And makes an application of them to her dearest friends,
Like a Good Old English Lady, of no particular Time.

She keeps a handsome equipage, and drives about in state,
But carefully avoids going through a Turnpike gate;
Not that she grudges paying, for her bounty is so great,
That some one saw her once at Church put sixpence in the Plate,
Like a fine Old English Lady, of no particular Time.

For she is truly liberal to her Ornaments and Dress,
And when some people call on her, with Tales of deep Distress
And ask for Contributions—she seldom does much less
Than say that though she never gives, she wishes them success,
Like a Good Old English Lady, of no particular Time.

And fearing too much sweetness might prove a cloying Drug,
If she makes her poor Companion's Life a somewhat weary Tug,
She balances asperities by extra-love to Pug,
That Darling, Snarling, Angel Dog, that lies upon the Rug,
Of this Good Old English Lady, of no particular Time.

When Death, who in his Regiment makes every one enlist,
Shall take this Pious Lady off, on one thing I insist,
Which is that go she where she may, she'll be extremely missed
By any Three who want a Fourth to take a hand at Whist,
Like a Good Old English Lady, of no particular Time.

SONG.

Tune—"THE DUSTY MILLER."

Never were such times,
Every thing so polished,
No one hears of Crimes,
For they have been abolished.
Vice, so people say,
Perfectly confounded
Lies in Schedule A,
Like a Donkey pounded.
   Never were such Times, &c.

If things seem the same
As before the Movement,
At least they 've changed their Name,
And that's a great improvement.
So let us quiet sit,
Whilst others Rob, and Rifle,
Felony is Wit,
Murder but a Trifle.
   Never were such Times, &c.

'T would scarcely win belief,
And, as to Feeling, shock it,
To hear him called a Thief,
Who only picks a Pocket.
Our Sages have defined
These little playful actions
Mere symptoms of a mind
Addicted to Abstractions.
   Never were such Times, &c.

Brownrigg, Cook, and Good!
Language almost falters
When vowing that you should
Have found no H-in Halters (Altars)
For in this Age of Gold,
Liberty, and Charters,
You must be enrolled
Among the blessed Martyrs.
                    Never were such Times, &c.

They stopped poor Brownrigg's breath
Because the honest Old Soul
Flogged three Girls to death
And hid them in a Coal Hole:
I'm sure there was no Sin
Or cruelty about her,
For when she crammed them in
She was no " Out and Outer,"
                    Never were such Times, &c.

Shew me in Ude's Book
Such a clever way as
That of the Great Cook
For dressing Mr. Pääs.
Ude would himself approve,
And own he never boasted
A more complete Remove,
Dished, Served out, and Roasted.
                    Never were such Times, &c.

Says friendly Good, his Guest
Politely thus addressing,
'Tis sweet in Peace to rest,

So I'll multiply the Blessing.
My love for you is such,
And hourly so increases,
That of you I'll make much,
And leave you all in Pieces.
   Never were such Times, &c.

Each Briton now maintains
His Privilege to Slaughter,
Knock out his Father's brains, '
And shoot his Wife, and Daughter.
If some old fashioned Dunce
Demands the Law's intrusion,
Physicians say at once,
'Tis " Innocent Delusion."
   Never were such Times, &c.

But as to my poor scull
I wish they would trepan it,
For I am far too dull
For our Improving Planet.
Some place would better please
Where none are daily frightened,
But all live more at ease
By being less Enlightened.
   Never were such Times,
   Every thing so polished,
   No one hears of Crimes,
   For they have been abolished.

A LAMENT.

———

In days like these, when Men and Things
  March on with fierce Improvement,
Poor Cupid mourns to find his Wings
  Won't flutter with the Movement.
For, Oh! the cruel Law steps in
  With unromantic blindness,
And with these words, " Too near of Kin,"
  Arrests the course of Kindness.
          With so few
          Left to woo
          What shall Women do!

Says Mary, "Oh! my heart is hot,
  And burnt as with a Blister,
Tom wants to wed me—but must not—
  I'm his Deceased Wife's sister.
He daily seeks for my consent,
  But fruitless quite the search is,
When wicked Acts of Parliament
  Stop axing in the Churches.
          Upon my word
          I never heard
          A Law half so absurd.

And pity, too, the Nephew's fate,
  Who spends his days a-grieving,
Because he's forced so long to wait
  For what his Aunt may leave him.

The same most wicked Act prevents,
  The wish of true affection
To gain her Heart and Three Per Cents,
  By Conjugal Connection.
        So he must wait
        And mourn his fate
        Quite disconsolate.

Oh! may our Parliament improve,
  And not allow to stand one
Bar between the Tender Love
  Of Grand-Mother and Grandson:
Then Love with Law no more will clash,
  And none their Passion smother,
But all with one harmonious hash
  May marry one another.
        Then shall we
        England see
        As it ought to be.

ON THE PLEASURES OF FURNISHING.

The Pastoral Poets may prate
Of Rural Retirement and Peace,
The Charms of so common a state
May do for a parcel of Geese.
In an age so enlightened as this,
These stupid ideas we'll drop,
And seek the Perfection of Bliss
Within an Upholsterer's Shop!

Then Ladies and Gentlemen haste,
Here's a summons that must be obeyed,
Remember to show you've a Taste,
And forget—there's a Bill to be paid.

But stop—for I must not neglect
My Orthography—have you not heard,
That Upholsterer is not correct,
But Upholder's the classical word:
And many may safely affirm,
Who have tasted of Bankruptcy's Cup,
How richly he merits the term,
Who has *done* them so properly *up*.
   Then Ladies and Gentlemen haste,
      &c. &c.

Who now would in Nature delight,
She plays such a trumpery part;
For nothing about her looks right
Without the assistance of Art.
The Winds seem to Whimper and Whine,
Where an ill-fitting Shutter is seen,
And the Sun to refuse us a Shine
Except through a Damask Moreen.
   So Ladies and Gentlemen haste,
      &c. &c.

Thus to Nature I cry, when my course
Lies through Scenes whose Sterility Shocks,
"Why hast thou so little Remorse,
And forgotten to furnish the Rocks!"
But when she is fruitful and kind,
And the Fields with her Flowers imprints

Her Colours recall to my mind
The superior charms of a Chintz.
  So Ladies and Gentlemen haste,
     &c. &c.

The dearest desire of my breast,
Were I cast on some desolate shore,
Would be, that I might be possest
Of a Carpet to cover the floor.
And in Deserts unfanned by a Breeze,
With checks fast beginning to singe,
I would think not of Verdure and Trees,
But sigh for a Curtain and Fringe.
  So Ladies and Gentlemen haste,
     &c. &c.

Sometimes I am destined to moan
When Cupid his favor withdraws,
And the Heart which I thought was my own
Is fast in an Ottoman's claws ;
And the Lady declares that she should
Before she can rashly presume
To judge if my Company's good,
Be better assured of my Room.
  So Ladies and Gentlemen haste,
     &c. &c.

What rapturous feelings entrance
When with Tones that remind of a Dove,
And quite an ecstatical glance,
She murmurs—" Oh! dear, what a Love !"
With equal excitement, I cry,
" Am I the blest Person you mean ?"

" No, Sir," is her tender reply,
" I meant, what a Love—of a Screen!"
   So Ladies and Gentlemen haste,
      &c. &c.

Our Laws, I assert it with pride,
No honors to Furniture grudge,
For we dare not on *Hangings* decide,
Unassisted by Jury and Judge.
And I'm sure, in one Branch of our State,
It has Representation enough,
For you'll find, when the Commons debate,
One half of them—Dealers in Stuff!
   So Ladies and Gentlemen haste,
      &c. &c.

See! some, by becoming a Board,
Their shattered Finances repair,
While Peace in the Senate's restored
By a solemn appeal to the Chair.
And the Prize most desired by those
Who seek no reward but renown,
Is being sworn in, to compose
A Cabinet fit for the Crown.
   So Ladies and Gentlemen haste,
      &c. &c.

If doomed to Misfortune, or Strife,
I'll bear them as meek as a Mouse,
I seek but one Blessing in Life,
And that is—to furnish my House.
May a Tomb-Stone, attesting my worth,
Record to my honor, when dead,

" Here is one who had nothing on earth
" Ill-furnished, excepting—his Head."
    So Ladies and Gentlemen haste,
    Here's a Summons that must be obeyed,
    Remember to show you 've a Taste,
    And forget—there's a Bill to be paid.

ON SIR ROBERT PEEL'S RECEPTION AT ABERDEEN.

Tell me the name I beg
    Of that Bonnie Chiel
Wie his Tartan and Philibeg?
    'Tis Sir Robert Peel.
Oh! Gude Sir Robert, say
    Where have you been?
" I have been far away
        At—Aberdeen."

What were you doing there?
    " I was getting Praise,
Getting what I've not, I swear,
    Had these many days.
For there they washed me with a flood
    Of Soap and Sawder, clean,
Scraping off the English Mud
        At—Aberdeen.

" I am tired of the stupid South,
    Where Farmers look so sad,

Declaring, with an angry mouth,
  That all is very bad.
In the clever North I feel
  A change of Note, and Scene,
From " very bad" to " varry weel"
          At—Aberdeen."

What did that douce and canny Man,
  The Provost, say to you?
" O! he said, that I was an
  Honest man and true.
His words were sweet, his Tongue was smooth,
  As his eyes were keen:
Provosts always speak the Truth
          At—Aberdeen.

" In the Town the joy was such,
  When I showed my Face,
I feel that Oxford is a much
  Inferior sort of place.
There they'd hoot, and make a noise,
  As soon as I was seen,
I saw no such naughty Boys
          At—Aberdeen."

Gude Sir Robert, maun I speir,
  Pray forgive the doubt,
Where will you go, if, as I fear,
  Your new Friends find you out!
If they should find out, that you say
  Not always what you mean,
Where will you go, if you can't stay
          At—Aberdeen.

"If they do such a horrid thing
    As to doubt my worth,
I must cut a Highland Fling
    And travel farther North
To the far, far North I'll go,
    I know no place between,
And live amongst the Esquimaux
                    Instead of—Aberdeen."

THE CAPTIVE.

Tune—"FILL THE BUMPER FAIR."

Fresh Lions yearly come,
    The Public Taste is pliant,
One year it takes Tom Thumb,
    And swallows next a Giant.
But "Forty six" has got
    The most uncommon Lion,
And serves him up quite hot,
    His name is Smith o'Brien.
                Hurrah! for Ireland's cause,
                    Hurrah for Ireland's Lion,
                Bad luck to sense, and laws;
                    Success to Smith O'Brien.

If a Lady should decline
    To come and see him, tell her,
That he'll soon be cool as Wine,
    For we keep him in the Cellar.
Walk down, then, without fear,
    And, what is most surprising,

Not only see—but hear
  Him thus soliloquising,
      "Hurrah for Ireland's cause,"
          &c. &c.

"Och! faith, I'm trapped and watched,
  And made a Blessed Martyr,
But I'll let them know they 've cotched
  A real Irish Tartar.
My Country will go mad,
  No mother's Son will fail her,
But every Irish Lad
  Start up a staunch Repaler.
      Hurrah! for Ireland's cause,
          &c. &c.

"The Gem of all the Sea
  Is half dissolved with weeping,
At a Gentleman like me
  In a Saxon Blackguard's keeping;
The best revenge, I think,
  For I cannot stoop to slay him,
Is to take his mate and drink,
  And take care—not to pay him.
      Hurrah! for Ireland's cause,
          &c. &c.

"The Saxons are well placed,
  When they to business muster,
But a Pathriot's disgraced
  By any thing but Bluster.
I'm not the cock to let
  A dirty Saxon Goose pull

My legs into the net
  Of doing something useful,
        Hurrah! for Ireland's cause,
            &c. &c.

" Confound the Spaker—Chair,
  Rules—Misures—Serjeants—Maces.
No Misures are so fair
  As Misures of twelve paces.
We'll keep our honour bright
  At tame Prescriptions scorning,
With Whisky Punch at night,
  And Pistols in the Morning.
        Hurrah! for Ireland's cause,
            &c. &c.

" When our Dis-uniting might
  Shall to Harmony restore us,
Och! Turf and Blitherumskite,
  We'll drive the World before us.
We'll break the Saxon rod,
  We'll spurn the Law's intrusion,
And keep our Verdant Sod
  Quite Sacred to Confusion.
        Hurrah! for Ireland's cause,
            &c. &c.

" When Ireland stands alone,
  Won't we be mighty clever,
Won't happiness unknown
  Reward the Land for ever.
Won't we, to shew the gains
  We get by Liberation,

Knock out each other's Brains
  In Paceful Agitation.
        Hurrah! for Ireland's cause,
                &c. &c.

" Though it's glorious here to rest,
  My Pathriot Zeal displaying,
Still I'd like that place the best,
  Which I was not forced to stay in—
I don't a Prison mind,
  Repalers do not doubt me,
But I fear the World may find
  It can get on without me.
        Hurrah for Ireland's cause,
                &c. &c.

" Once out, away I'll jog,
  And scorn the Speaker's Summons,
And I'll back an Irish Bog
  Against the British Commons.
Should a Missinger annoy,
  Deep down in some Turf-Pit, he
Will know I aint the Boy
  To serve on a Committee.
        Hurrah! for Ireland's Cause,
         Hurrah! for Ireland's Lion,
        Bad luck to sense, and laws,
         Success to Smith O'Brien."

"THE REPEALER."

Tune—" GROVES OF BLARNEY."

I'm a bold Repaler, and there's not a gentaler,
  Or more wholesale daler, in Seditious Stuff,
And in Beautiful Spaches, inducing Braches
  Of ugly Peace, of which we've had enough.
For, Och!—Stimulation to Separation,
  And Liberation, is my pride and joy,
And for bold attacks on the Bloody Saxon,
  When Words alone are wanted, I'm the Boy.

Och! when before ye I lay the Story
  Of the Gains and Glory ye'll get by a Divorce,
Faith! your eyes would glisten, if you'd only listen,
  And believe one Quarter of what I shall discourse.
No more Ploughing, or Sowing, or Reaping, or Mowing,
  No more Servants going, at their Masters call,
But of nothing else thinking, but fighting and drinking,
  Sure won't we then be Gintlemen any how at all?

We'll give a hiding to the Saxons for riding
  On poor old Ireland's back this many a day,
Like Divel's Postillions, and robbing us of Millions,
  Which we're good enough to owe them, & don't intend
For we will be laving off all, except recaving,   [to pay.
  And forget the word " Debt," by gineral consint,
But I won't be objecting to your now and then collecting
  For a Pathriot Repaler, like myself, a little Rint.

Och! won't we be frisky when the rivers run with Whisky,
   And the purling brooks soft Buttermilk distil,
When a swate Diffusion of Gineral Confusion
   Proclaims that Irish Pathriots are doing what they will.
When with hands in the bottom of our Pockets, (if we've
      got 'em,)
   We'll be feeling for the Thirteens, which we hope we
      may find there ;
If not, we'll try another's, for, shan't we all be Brothers ?
   And nobody have nothing, and every one a share ?

Lest sad remimbrance should be a hindrance
   And make the Patient soul of Ireland fret,
Whate'er we borrow—before the morrow
   The same we will be mindful to forget.
Then Collectors, and Excisemen, will not be very wise men,
   As we fairly advertise them, if their ugly Mugs they show.
For with good Shillalah whacks 'tis, we'll be settling all
      the Taxes,
   And give, with Pistol practice, a discharge for what
      we owe.

Now, after such a Sarmint, you'll be nothing else but
      varmint,
   If you don't at once detarmine the Irish coast to clear,
For the sake of dis-uniting, don't mind a little fighting,
   Which I take a great delight in, if it does not come too
But, as a bullet, flying, will take no denying,   [near ;
   But, in my poor Brain prying, might have a mind to stay,
For my own satisfaction, upon the day of Action,
   Faith ! 'tis Myself, I think, will keep away.

ON THE PAPAL AGGRESSION.

Oh! what can the matter be, Murder or Battery,
Has the Bull broken in to the best China shop,
Is it Felony?—Treason?—Do tell me the reason,
For its all botheration from bottom to top?
Who is it?—who is it?—who pays us a visit?
It is not the real Sea-Serpent I hope,
So frisky and frantic—fresh from the Atlantic?
Oh! No! 'tis that deeper Old Serpent the Pope.
 We are all in a quiver, for who shall deliver
 From Fire and Faggot—from Halter and Rope,
 The whole English Nation, is under invasion,
 And is going to be quickly devoured by the Pope.

Good People are crying—'Tis time to be flying,
We're ready to go to the North or the South,
For here we are undone—The Pope is in London,
And staying they say at the Bull and the Mouth.
Oh! he'll eat us, and floor us,—He'll toss us, and gore us,
In vain from his Clutches we try to elope,
For wherever we be, Sir—at Breakfast or Tea, there
Hot Water will always be served by the Pope.
 We are all in a quiver—for who shall deliver, &c. &c.

Oh! he'll catch and trepan us, perhaps he'll Japan us,
And alter us so, that each person will cry,
As he under-goes his—new metempsychosis,
"'Tis somebody else, for it cannot be I."
Due Patience and Vigour may whiten a Nigger,
And mend his Complexion with Brushes and Soap,

But Fifty-Horse power, applied every hour,
Won't take off the Varnish laid on by the Pope.
　　　We are all in a quiver, for who shall deliver, &c. &c.

Large Hat, and Red Stocking, and all that is shocking,
We think of by day—and we dream of by Night :
Oh ! he's a bold traitor, there can't be a greater,
Who dares not to be in a terrible fright.
Poor famishing Sinners won't ring for their Dinners,
They can't read a Book, and in Darkness they Grope,
For no one dares handle a Bell, Book, or Candle,
The thought of such things so reminds of the Pope.
　　　We are all in a quiver, for who shall deliver, &c. &c.

To quell the Seditious, tell all the Militias,
The Clerks, and Churchwardens, to come to our aid,
And bid the Exciseman charge Cardinal Wiseman,
And keep him away till the Duty is paid.
My Lord Mayor have Pity, and make the whole City
Turn out, with this Foreign Marauder to cope ;
Do not unwilling wait—Ladies of Billingsgate,
Help with your Tongues in defying the Pope.
　　　We are all in a quiver, for who shall deliver, &c. &c.

Excuse me for saying—by way of delaying,
My Friends, your most Pious and Orthodox fear,
That I have a Receipt here—there's not a completer,
To drive the Pope off—though its rather severe.
Stick to him like Leeches—with very long speeches,
Give your Lungs, and your Tongues, and your Eloquence scope,

et him pass but one Week in the hearing you Speaking,
nd you'll not get a visit again from the Pope.
    We're all in a quiver, for who shall deliver
    From Fire and Faggot—from Halter and Rope ;
    The whole English Nation is under invasion,
    And is going to be quickly devoured by the Pope.

BARNEY MAGUIRE.

(On the Launch of the Windsor Castle *at* Pembroke Dock,
afterwards re-named "The Duke of Wellington.")

    Poor Barney Maguire, who's
    Extremely desirous
Of seeing all Wonders from London to Cork,
    Permission is craving,
    That through Milford Haven
You'll kindly allow him to take a short walk.
    And he cannot do less, Sir,
    Than freely confess, Sir,
That what he has seen there completely outstrips.
    With proud Emulation
    The Great Coronation,
And that is the Launch of the Biggist of Ships.
    'Tis Curious, reelly,
    To see how Genteely,
And freely, from Land into Water she slips ;
    There's noting in Natur
    That ever can bate her,
The Illigant Cratur, the Biggist of Ships.

This New Windsor Castle
Has clearly surpassed all
The Fame of the Old one, that stands on dry Ground,
For would it not smother,
Or bother the other,
To walk through the Water without getting drowned.
This says to the Dry Land,
Politely, "Good Bye"—and
All over the Waves, like a Didapper, skips,
Sure a grave Turk, or Persian,
Might laugh with diversion,
At seeing the Launch of the Biggist of Ships.
'Tis Curious, reelly,
&c. &c.

The Winds, so contrary,
That constantly vary,
Will find her too wary, so little she cares
For them, or their Bellows,
The impudent Fellows,
When giving themselves, and not others, their airs.
If they stop Loco-motion
Upon the Wide Ocean,
She'll sarve out Promotion to one who quite whips
The Winds—'tis the Stoker,
Who'll come with his Poker,
And get up the Steam for the Biggist of Ships.
'Tis Curious, reelly,
&c. &c.

But when she is sailing,
Each Porpoise, and Whale, in
A Wonder will cry, " Who is coming to call ?
If she's got Relations,

Two such visitations
Will make the Wide Ocean too small for us all.
And that Heathenish Varmint
The Famous Sea-Sarpint
Will scarcely determine—whilst licking his lips,
The delicate question,
If his Digestion
Fairly can deal with the Biggist of Ships."
'Tis Curious, reelly,
&c. &c.

See! how well she's obeyed all
Commands in the Cradle,
When ordered she's off, and there can't be a doubt,
That nothing will stop her,
Whilst all is so proper,
That her Mother who christened must know she is Out.
Och! I'm three parts delighted,
And just one affrighted,
And half my poor senses are in an Eclipse;
So, Faith, I am thinking,
'Tis time to be Drinking
Success, and Long Life, to the Biggist of Ships.
'Tis Curious, reelly,
To see how Genteely
And freely from Land into Water she slips.
Oh! there's nothing in Natur
That ever can bate her
The illigant Cratur, the Biggist of Ships.

On the Breaking up of LORD ABERDEEN'S
Government, and upon MR. ROEBUCK'S Motion.

Tune—" WILLIKINS AND HIS DINAH."

An Omnibus lately in London was seen,
    Which carried some Servants, who lived with the Queen,
So Flash a concern, that it never set down,
    Or took any one up, but in Windsor or Town.
        Singing toorala toorala toorala la.

Some say that these Servants were such a nice set,
    That they all pulled together whenever they met,
Whilst others (though I don't believe it) suppose,
    That the pull they best liked was of each other's nose;
        Singing toorala toorala toorala la.

Now the Coachman who drove had been young long ago,
    And some thought him Steady and some only Slow,
And he was assisted by a knowing lad,
    Who once had been Coachman, but now was turned Cad.
        Singing toorala toorala toorala la.

This Cad used to say, with a very smooth face,
    That he much preferred the inferior Place,
And that nothing on earth gave him so much delight,
    As to stand on the footboard, and cry out, " All Right."
        Singing toorala toorala toorala la.

But he was a deep one, who knew now to fib,
    For finding the Horses one day stand and jib,
At the sign of the Roebuck off slily he steals,
    And pulls all the Linchpins right out of the Wheels,
        Singing toorala toorala toorala la.

Then, as soon as they started, he jumps from the Board,
  For he likes to get others, but not himself, floored,
And sees the poor Omnibus suddenly pitch
  The Servants and Driver slap into the Ditch.
             Singing toorala toorala toorala la.

The Flunkeys they swore, but the Cad said, " don't doubt
  That I've made you fall in, that you may not fall out,
And to prove that the best of you cannot approach
  Little John in the art of upsetting the Coach."
             Singing toorala toorala toorala la.

Moral.

Here's a warning no Omnibus Driver should scoff,
  Let him look to his Linchpins before he sets off,
And Omnibus Owners henceforth will be mad,
  When they turn off a Coachman, to keep him as Cad.
             Singing toorala toorala toorala la.

REBECCA.
On the South Wales Turnpike Gate Riots in 1843, generally called " Rebecca Riots."

Rebecca's Soirées extort my Praise
  Her kindness never abates,
She goes out by night her friends to invite,
  And she Axes all the Gates.
Oh ! she is as bold, as an Amazon of old,
  For it is her constant boast,
A la militaire, that she can't bear
  Ever to leave a Post.

So Saw, and Smash, and out with your Cash,
 And never mind what's to pay,
But kick up a dust, and down with the Trust,
 And that's your Time of Day.

Here's a valuable truth for a love-sick youth,
 Who is caught by Rebecca's Charms,
She's a Widow, and free, as any need be,
 Both of her hands and arms.
But, I fear, as a wife, she'd trouble his life,
 For she's something of a Scold,
And always inclined to tell her own mind
 But cannot bear being *Toll'd.*
   So Saw, and Smash, and out with your Cash,
          &c. &c.

Rebecca has got a charming lot
 Of Daughters to bring out,
And thinks no place, like Ball, or Race,
 So fit as a Midnight Rout;
Young Ladies, like these, are of course hard to please,
 But still, I think, if *courted*
By the judging Few, who would give them their Due,
 They would be all Transported.
   So Saw, and Smash, and out with your Cash,
          &c. &c.

Now if any enquire, what there is to inspire
 Dislike, or so infringes
On the Quiet of her nerves, when Rebecca observes
 A Gate upon all its hinges?
Now I'll tell you why, and a truer reply
 Was never yet said, or sung,

She reads her Fate in a Turnpike Gate,
  Or any thing else that's hung.
    So Saw, and Smash, and out with your Cash,
      And never mind what's to pay,
    But kick up a dust, and down with the Trust,
      And that's your Time of Day.

A WELSH ODE.

COMPOSED FOR THE EISTEDDFOD.

My Friends, and Dear Countrymen, do not discard,
  The Song and advice of a Patriot Bard,
Who wants you to listen to Cambria's praise,
  To keep up old Customs, and walk in old ways,
    So snug in Humbugging, and Tomfoolery.

For why should our Bodies or minds ever roam,
  When both can be furnished so sweetly at Home,
Why trammel our arms, like the Saxons, with Coats,
  And not live unencumbered with Clothes, like the Goats,
    So snug in Humbugging, and Tomfoolery.

I wish you to spurn Foreign Food, Dress, and Laws,
  To breakfast on Hips—and to dine upon Haws,
Why traffic with Sheffield, when taught by the Hawks,
  Not to live with ten Fingers dependent on Forks.
    So snug in Humbugging, and Tomfoolery.

And why should you sums so extravagant pay,
  To know what one Shakespeare, or Milton, may say,

When we can have, fresh from the Land of our Birth,
Penillions for nothing, and at their true worth :
    So snug in Humbugging, and Tomfoolery.

Can Wellington with Twm Shon Catty compare,
  Or the Heroes who lived, no one knows when or where,
And as to comparing Lord Nelson, 'tis gammon
  To a Celt in a Coracle, fishing for Salmon :
    So snug in Humbugging, and Tomfoolery.

Whenever I look at an Apple, I grieve
  To think of the Tree that so tempted poor Eve,
And feel she would not have been led to such freaks,
  If, instead of the Apples, the Tree had borne Leeks :
    So snug in Humbugging, and Tomfoolery.

Geologists tell us our Land was quite free
  From the waters, when Europe was half under sea,
Then what Demonstration more clear can you wish,
  That we were fine Fellows, when Saxons were Fish !
    So snug in Humbugging, and Tomfoolery.

If there be amongst you one vile Saxon Knave hid,
  Pray, knock out his brains in the name of St. David.
And our Land will, when there's not a stranger to pelt,
  Be the Land of perfection, the Land of the Celt,
    So snug in Humbugging, and Tomfoolery.

My Song would be longer, but I have my fears,
  It wants a fit Audience with much longer Ears,
With much longer Ears to take in all my Tales,
  And to vibrate with joy to the Praises of Wales,
    So snug in Humbugging, and Tomfoolery.

THE FINE YOUNG ENGLISH LADY.

Tune—"THE FINE OLD ENGLISH GENTLEMAN."

———

I'll sing you a new song, if you'll condescend to wait,
 Of a fine young English Lady, neither solemn, nor sedate,
But one who can do every thing at a very rapid rate,
 Sing, Dance, Quadrille, and Galloppade, and sometimes
         flirt and prate,
  Like a fine young English Lady, one of the present time.

Her nerves are often very weak, more often still her head,
 So she lies, and takes pretty good Supplies of Tea and
         Toast, in Bed,
Then comes down late to Breakfast, and is pleased to
         here it said,
 That she must be a Sylphide, who on air alone is fed,
  Like a fine young English Lady, one of the present time.

To prove her Genius she displays her Drawings, or unwraps
 A roll of the sweetest Patterns for Bonnets, Gowns, & Caps,
Or, after much entreaty, (for she's diffident,) perhaps,
 She'll shew you her little Album full of sentimental scraps,
  Like a fine young English Lady, one of the present time.

She loves romantic incidents, if set to a soft tune,
 And talks of Love in Lapland, when warm at home in June ;
Or, when seated by the fire of a Winter's afternoon,
 Avows a most astonishing affection for the Moon,
  Like a fine young English Lady, one of the present time.

Her sensibility is great, and many tears distills,
 O'er the sorrows of poor Werter, and her milliner's long Bills,

And what Papa will say to them, her mind with Terror fills,
　For the Figures are far less pleasing than those of the new
　　　　　　　　　　　　Quadrilles,
　　To this fine young English Lady, one of the present time.

She writes one Ode to Solitude, another to Despair,
　And vows that Crowds, and the sight of Men, are more than
　　　　　　　　　　　her nerves can bear,
So of course no other motive, but exercise and air,
　Makes her ride in the Park, at half past five, when all the
　　　　　　　　　　　World is there,
　　Like a fine young English Lady, one of the present time.

But, if you are her Confidante, her sorrows she unlocks,
　And talks of Cruel Fathers, with hearts as hard as rocks,
Who, while they squander Hundreds in following a fox,
　Are deaf to the claims of Nature, and refuse an Opera Box
　　To a fine young English Lady, one of the present time.

For the Opera is so superior to a stupid Play or Ball,
　And those dear Italian singers her senses so enthrall,
That it must be the merest Accident, if a few soft glances fall
　On some well-moustachioed Dandy, who is lounging in his stall,
　　From this fine young English Lady, one of the present time.

And sometimes she will moralize, and softly sigh, " Alas!
　How true it is that we all must fade, like the flowers
　　　　　　　　　　　of the Grass."
And vowing that each moment shall in Self-improvement pass,
　Devotes a quiet hour to Reflection—in the Glass,
　　Like a fine young English Lady, one of the present time.

Now in these Employments, interpersed with Dejeuners
and Drives,
This excellent young Person to pass her time contrives,
And if all her Fair Companions thus regulate their lives,
Why then our fine young Gentlemen will find the best
of Wives,
In the fine young English Ladies, those of the present time.

---

*Yesterday a Cabbage of the Drum-Head Species was cut in the
Garden of J. H. Philipps, Esq. of Williamstone, measuring
......feet in Circumference.* (Local Paper.)

Tune—" GROVES OF BLARNEY."

Oh! the Groves of the Blarney would no longer
charm ye,
But a poor Consarn ye would call them sure enough,
Nor worth one Farden, could you see my Garden,
Where grow potatoes, and sweet kitchen stuff;
Oh! 'tis the station for fine vegetation,
And young plantations, Sucker, Shrub, and Shoot,
And Peach trees blooming, though they are not
presuming,
And far too modest to bear any fruit.

Oh! 'tis an action of great satisfaction,
My feet on beds of sweet Herbs to imprint,
In full Fruition of my proud position,
As Lord of Thyme and Master of Mint.
And in the Alleys, oh! should any Malice,
Come between Man and Wife, when walking there,

And make them Quarrel, they may learn a Moral,
　From seeing still an undivided *Pear*.

You'd be enchanted at beholding planted,
　The Bashful Carrot, blushing rosy red,
And long Cucumber, the lazy lumber,
　A lying all day long on his Hot-Bed.
And there's the glory of my Grounds and story,
　Whose worth beats praise and makes description mean,
So Mr. Babbage may survey my Cabbage,
　And find its value by his new Machine.

Should any wonder, when they 're standing under
　His Lordly Head, what makes it rise so high,
I'm proud to mention, 'tis the kind intention
　Of helping Nature brushing clean the sky.
For which, a share he has of her great Dairy,
　Though t'aint with Crame he's paid, but mere Sky-blue,
Nor will he let her long remain his Debtor,
　Since every evening he receives his Dew.

If for dissection you 've a Predilection,
　And would inspect his great Anatomy,
You'd say his juices did exceed the Sluices,
　Which save all Holland from going out to Sea.
So thick his shade is, that 'twill keep a Lady's
　Complexion safe from fiery sun and moon,
And be a shelter, where no storm can pelt her,
　When "drinking Tea" there of the afternoon.

But now, see muster an admiring cluster
　Of Swine, and other Contemplative Bastes,
Who show their Larning, by discourse consarning
　What most would please their individual tastes.

One Pig is wishing, they may not be dishing
  His Comely person with the dirty Beans,
But hopes, when salted, he may be exalted,
  And served as Bacon to his Worship's Greens.

The Ox advances with contemptuous glances,
  And Lordly indignation in his face,
And says, " you Blackguard, stay in Sty, or Haggard,
  For here you are entirely out of place.
I am much mistaken, if it is with Bacon
  The King of Greens would combination seek,
When he'll gain double honor, if I'm Bubble,
  And sing a Second to his First, as Squeak."

But now the Cabbage, getting rather savage,
  Says, " This same noise a'int decent, or well bred,
If you're not quiet, I must end the Riot
  By a Court Martial held on my Drum Head.
His aspiration for Publication
  In Leaves of mine the Pig shall not fulfil,
And let North meet South 'ere the Bull and Mouth, there,
  Shall sing with me the Great Green Man and Still."

And now is there not any Professor, here, of Botany,
  Who knows all Cabbages, by Nature, and by Name,
To take up my Song and mend it, for I myself must end it,
  Since I am quite tired with hammering on the same.
And Oh ! I'd be delighted, if you'd think yourselves
      invited
  To come to My House, and see this Raree show,
Which, you'd all be agreeing, was a sight worth the
      seeing,
  Only—it was cut down six months ago !

WHIST.

Tune—"*There's nae luck about the House.*"

I have roamed the world for Pleasure,
    But it came not at my call,
And I vainly sought the treasure
    At Opera and Ball.
And this is the conclusion
    My Reason can't resist,
All pleasure is Delusion
    Except a Game at Whist.
        So what care I, for Wet, or Dry,
          For Sunshine, Moon, or Mist,
          For Day, or Night, so I have light
          Enough to play at Whist.

I love to see, in solemn State,
    Four grave Professors meet,
Who waste no time in dull debate,
    Like Men in Downing Street,
Each careful not a word to say,
    Lest partners should revoke,
For they know their business is to Play,
    And such Play is no Joke.
        So what care I, for Wet, or Dry, &c.

Should little murmurs reach your ears,
    Or rude remarks arise,
And make you fear a quarrel near,
    Don't trust your ears or eyes.
For how disputes should intervene,
    I cannot understand,

Between four People, who are seen
 To sit with Hand in Hand.
   So what care I, for Wet, or Dry, &c.

If Chartists in our Streets are seen,
 Or Rebels wildly rave,
There's peace at Whist, where King and Queen
 Can always beat the Knave.
And at the Cards we seldom swear,
 For what would be the use,
Of saying, "the Deuce take them," where
 Every one can take the Deuce.
   So what care I, for Wet, or Dry, &c.

In that delighted Lady's face,
 When fortune smiles upon her,
The Soul of Chivalry I trace,
 She prizes so her Honor.
But ah! some feelings of regret
 With satisfaction mix,
When I find, though fond of Honors, yet,
 She'd rather win by Tricks.
   So what care I, for Wet, or Dry, &c.

Lord Eglinton's best Knights must feel,
 Whilst envy strikes them mute,
That not their brightest Coat of Steel
 Can match our Diamond Suit.
We fight all night, yet none are worse,
 For all escape disaster,
When Points can only pierce the Purse,
 And Cutting needs no plaster.
   So what care I, for Wet, or Dry, &c.

D

The wisest of Physicians,
  Whose name will Long endure,
Prescribed, for all Conditions,
  A Rubber, as a Cure.
And thinking mere Prescribing wrong,
  If Practice is not taught,
With his Bills he played a game at Long,
  With his Patients' Lives at Short.
            So what care I, for Wet, or Dry, &c.

The Youth, by frantic Love possest,
  May talk of Flames, and Darts,
And swear he's Master of the Best,
  So of course the Ace of Hearts.
But the Heart of no fond lover
  With such Palpitation jumps,
As mine, when I discover
  That I've got the Ace of Trumps.
            So what care I, for Wet, or Dry, &c.

When age shall sap my feeble frame,
  And strength, and health get slack,
I still can find at Home my Game,
  And Hunt with my own Pack.
And when seated at my Rubber,
  I will not be afraid
Of a Chartist with a Club, or
  A Sexton with a Spade.
            So what care I, for Wet, or Dry,
              For Sunshine, Moon, or Mist,
            For Day, or Night, so I have light
              Enough to play at Whist.

WEDDING SONG.

Tune—"FILL THE BUMPER FAIR."

———

Sing a Marriage Strain,
  Let the Glasses jingle,
Half, and Half we'll drain,
  Nothing now is Single.
See the Fast ones run,
  See the slow ones carried,
All, both Old, and Young,
  Going to be Married.
      Sing a Marriage Strain,
        Let your Glasses jingle,
      Half, and Half we'll drain,
        Nothing now is Single.

O'Connell now would feel
  In a shocking passion,
For 'tis vain to preach Repeal,
  When Union's so in fashion.
Neuters even drop
  Their former appellation,
And run to Hymen's shop
  For soft Concatenation.
      Sing a Marriage Strain, &c. &c.

All Looks, here below,
  Wear Love's Magic traces,
Clocks and Watches show
  Something Moving in their Faces.
But Time forbids their Banns,
  Disputing Hymen's power,

And says, "Don't give your Hands,
   For you'll want them every Hour."
       Sing a Marriage Strain, &c. &c.

Cupid brags, and boasts,
   That nothing says to him "Nay,"
Spits wound the Hearts of Roasts,
   Smoke-Jack flirts with Chimney,
Fire-Irons do not wait,
   But tumble soon in Love all,
Fender grins at Grate,
   And Poker smirks at Shovel.
       Sing a Marriage Song, &c. &c.

Cheeses can't escape
   The tender passion sharing,
But they go through many a Scrape,
   Before there is much Paring.
One Couple I must praise,
   Who sounder notions foster,
And live, from earliest days,
   A steady Double Glos'ter.
       Sing a Marriage Strain, &c. &c.

Some with Love seem drunk;
   For, an Oil-Skin Cover
Took an old Hair-Trunk
   As her accepted Lover.
How he stormed, and raged,
   When after him she ran, to
Say she was engaged
   To a smart Portmanteau.
       Sing a Marriage Strain, &c. &c.

Of a Table's Charms
  A Chair enamoured rushes,
Crying, " In my Arms
  Hide your modest blushes."
" Can you, Sir, sustain
  The burthen," says the Table,
" Because, if you are Cane, (Cain)
  I'm sure you are not Able." (Abel)
        Sing a Marriage Strain, &c. &c.

And now I must intrude
  A wish in this last stanza,
And I will so conclude,
  My Extravaganza.
May each Man love his Wife,
  Each Wife be never jealous,
United both for life,
  Like a pair of Tongs, or Bellows.
      Sing a Marriage Strain,
        Let the glasses jingle,
      Half, and Half we'll drain,
        Nothing, now, is Single.

THE RESPECTABLE MAN.

Through life would you easily glide,
  Or start for the Sweepstakes of Fame,
Believe me you never can ride,
  Such a Capital Horse as a Name.

And if there be one to surpass
　All others that ever yet ran,
Like Eclipse, in a Match with an Ass,
　'Tis the ' Highly Respectable Man.'

Don't ask me, I beg, to explain;
　The order I cannot obey;
What meaning the words may contain,
　I have not the presumption to say:
But I know that no Rogue's at a loss,
　If he has but the moral Japan,
The plumage, and exquisite Gloss,
　Of the ' Highly Respectable Man.'

There is Mr. Bamboozle, whose ways
　All those who deal with him bewitch,
Each goes away poor, whilst he stays
　Of course most unconsciously rich.
If I should presume to suspect,
　The answer is " Oh! Sir, how can
You dare one bad thought to connect
　With that ' Highly Respectable Man.'

Captain Do'em-all, clever, and smart,
　With an innocent smile on his face,
Has a very particular art
　Of playfully Cutting an Ace.
If I wish young beginners to warn,
　Lest he the unwary trepan,
All cry, " Imputations we scorn
　On that ' Highly Respectable Man.'

There is Mr. Softsawder, 'tis said,
　And it's hard to refute it, contrives,

By his skilful arrangements, to wed
  Quite a Turkish assortment of Wives.
But the Ladies, attesting his worth,
  With a Blush, that half fires a Fan,
Cry " If there's an Angel on Earth,
  'Tis that Highly Respectable Man."

Some-times, when I venture to buy,
  And a Bill for the payment is sent,
Where I find all the charges too high,
  By nearly five hundred per cent.
I am told, " Sir, I take it quite ill
  That the items you venture to scan,
Low Charges become not the Bill
  Of a ' Highly Respectable Man.'

To my rather obdurate mind
  'Tis really quite a relief,
When-ever I happen to find
  A thorough professional Thief,
Of such I am not much afraid,
  But should tremble, if once he began
To quit his old Tricks, for the Trade
  Of a ' Highly Respectable Man.'

And now, since my Rhapsody ends,
  I hope that you are not too nice
To take in the shape of amends,
  A small piece of wholesome advice :
If the right from the wrong you'd divide,
  And sift it, like flour from bran,
Put it quite on the opposite side
  Of the ' Highly Respectable Man.'

THE FRENCH REVOLUTION, 1848.

Tune—" THE KING OF THE CANNIBAL ISLANDS."

———

Ourselves—Our noble Selves we'll praise,
  For getting up such glorious Days,
And shewing the World the best of ways
    To mend a Constitution.
We told our King—old Louis Philippe,
  We're wide awake—you're fast a-sleep,
And though you think yourself so deep,
  You are not the Shepherd for such fast Sheep:
    For we'll do nothing, but cry "Victoire,
      Chanter—Changer—Manger—Boire,
    What fine supplies of Gammon, and Gloire
    Are got by a Revolution.

We'll force all Tyrants to resign,
  Who wont allow the people to dine,
And teach the world—by drinking Wine,
    To mend a Constitution.
We'll give the Congè to Guizot,
  And say to Odillon Barrott,
" The pace our watches have learnt to go,
  Make all your movements much too slow,
    For we'll do nothing, but cry " Victoire," &c.

A bright example we will set,
  That none at another's loss should fret,
For to keep what we get, and pay no Debt.
    Is to mend the Constitution.

And to prove that a Frenchman's soul's above
  Ill Will, and as gentle as a Dove,
If away the English workman we shove,
    We'll keep their Money to prove our Love.
        For we'll do nothing, but cry " Victoire," &c.

As we want Supplies we should think it strange
  If you object to what we arrange,
As a very Charming mode of Exchange,
    To mend our Constitution.
You shall give us your Money, and take our thanks,
  If not, you may quit the Patriot Ranks,
And we'll shew you some pretty National Pranks,
  By taking French leave, and your Cash in the Banks.
        For we'll do nothing, but cry " Victoire," &c.

If any of Sense, and Justice, prate,
  We'll force such things to Abdicate,
They do not suit our improving State,
    Which mends its Constitution.
We will make it appear, as clear as the Moon,
  That Nations must dance to another Tune,
As Monsieur Arago will find very soon,
  By laws discovered in the Moon.
        For we'll do nothing, but cry " Victoire," &c.

And now we'll try, and count the Gains
  We've got by taking so much pains,
And blowing out each others Brains,
    To mend a Constitution.
Negation's Triumph is complete,
  For we've nothing to do, but to walk in the street,

With no Clothes on our Backs, no Shoes on our Feet,
  With Nothing to Drink, and Nothing to Eat;
        And though we shout, and cry, " Victoire,"
          'Tis Changer, without any Manger, Boire,
          For more Supplies of Gammon, than Gloire,
          Are got by a Revolution.

———

THE DESERTED PARISH.

Tune—" How Happy could I be with either."

———

We send you a Humble Petition,
    We hope you won't take it amiss,
For never was yet the Condition
    Of any poor Parish like this.
We've not got a Parson a-near us,
    To tell us a Stick from a Star ;
To keep our poor heads straight, and cheer us,
    By saying what Sinners we are.
            And 'tis Oh ! Dear, we must enquire,
              Oh ! dear, what we're to do,
            If you will not come any nigher,
              Or the Parish go no nigher to you

The Lamb may lie down with the Leopard,
    The Mice with the Kitten may play,
But the Sheep, that have not got a Shepherd,
    Must be in a very bad way.
The Parson, who goes from his people,
    And leaves his poor flock in the lurch,

Is just all the same as the Steeple
   A-walking away from the Church.
       And 'tis, Oh! Dear, we must enquire, &c.

We are like an old Coach, full of Cracks, all
   Our Wheels are beginning to Creak,
With no Oil, and with no Patent Axle,
   To make them run on for the week.
Though the Body may take a fair polish,
   When scrubbed on a Saturday night,
If you won't light the Lamps of our Knowledge,
   Oh! how can the Guard say " All right."
       And 'tis Oh! Dear, we must enquire, &c.

When the Parson's not ready for Lovers,
   They get rather awkward to please,
And each, before Marriage discovers
   There's time for a bit of a Breeze.
They live, then, like two empty Barrels,
   Quite void of all Spirit, and Strife;
For they've skimmed off the Cream of their Quarrels
   Before they are made Man, and Wife.
       And 'tis, Oh! Dear, we must enquire, &c.

And now, we must beg you to listen
   To what would put Saints in a rage,
Before the poor Infants we christen,
   They're very near dead of Old Age.
All's as slow as a man who is wherried
   Against a foul wind and strong tide,
For we wait such a time to be Buried,
   We had almost as soon not have Died.
       And 'tis, Oh! Dear, we must enquire, &c.

And now, Sir, we hope that this letter
  Won't leave you the less of a Friend,
Because you find nothing that's better
  Than Compliments put at the End.
But no one knows better, than you, the
  Reason why such is the Case,
We can't send you our Service, and Duty,
  For you give us none in the Place,
      And 'tis, Oh! Dear, we must enquire,
        Oh! dear, what shall we do,
      If you will not come any nigher,
        Or the Parish go nigher to you.

SIR ROBERT PEEL.

Tune—"LUCY NEAL."

I was bred in a Protection School,
  And always taught to feel,
That there was no one fit to rule,
  Except Sir Robert Peel.
For he shewed such deep affection
  For our Mutton, Beef, and Veal,
That I said "If there's Perfection
  In the World, 'tis Robert Peel.
    Oh! Sir Robert Peel, Oh! Sir Robert Peel,
      When you was voting by my side,
    How happy did I feel.

When Bright, or Cobden, made a speech,
  I turned upon my heel,

And said, "I've left a match for each
   In good Sir Robert Peel."
For no one fights for all the rights
   Of our Flour, and Barley Meal,
And fondly doats on native Oats,
    Like dear Sir Robert Peel.
     Oh! Sir Robert Peel; Oh! Sir Robert Peel:
      When you were voting by my side,
     How happy did I feel.

One Morn there came some horrid News,
   It almost made me reel,
That poor Protection's Ships, and Crews,
   Were cut by Robert Peel.
So instead of swimming with the Flood,
   I flounder like an Eel;
For I'm left sticking in the mud
   By sly Sir Robert Peel.
     Oh! Sir Robert Peel; Oh! Sir Robert Peel:
      You've cut, and shuffled all the Pack,
     And made a horrid Deal.

I don't know what he's thinking,
   But the wound he cannot heal,
For my Rents, my Rents, are sinking
   On account of Robert Peel;
And when I get from bad to worse,
   And am forced to pick, and steal,
I'll say " 't ain't I, vot prigs the Purse,
   But 'tis Sir Robert Peel."
     Oh! Sir Robert Peel; Oh! Sir Robert Peel:
      I shall owe you a good turn,
     When I'm on the Tread-Wheel.

E

THE VICTIM.

Tune—"THE FAIREST FLOWER."

I'm a very harmless man,
  Who do the best I can
Not to give the World pretence
  To take the least offence;
So I really do not know
  Why the Ladies use me so,
That I am forced, against my will,
  To dance in a Quadrille.
      A little Quadrille, a quiet Quadrille,
  A little, very far from merry, quiet Quadrille.

I'm not at all at ease,
  When dancing the Trenise,
And look a perfect fool,
  Advancing in La Poule,
And as to the Eté,
  Why, all that I can say
Is, "I feel even Summer-chill,
  When it comes in a Quadrille."
      A little Quadrille, a quiet Quadrille, &c.

By the Lancers 'tis my luck
  To be the first that's stuck,
And though my feelings bleed,
  To stop I can't succeed.
I say "I don't know how;"
  Still the Ladies won't allow
Me to go away, until
  They have finished the Quadrille.
      A little Quadrille, a quiet Quadrille, &c.

I submit to Ladies charms
　Without a Chaine de Dames,
And, their merits well to weigh,
　Don't want to "Balancer,"
But their Chassées I must blame,
　And wish they would find game
Elsewhere to hunt, and kill,
　But not in a Quadrille,
　　In a little Quadrille, a quiet Quadrille, &c.

And oh! when I am dead,
　With a Tombstone at my head,
An Inscription there you'll view
　Of H. D. O. A. Q.
If you'd know what this may mean,
　And what should come between,
The spaces you may fill
　With, " He died of a Quadrille:"
　　Of a little Quadrille, a quiet Quadrille,
A little, very *far* from merry, quiet Quadrille.

THE DUTY OF MAN.

Tune—..................

The lesson that I give,
　If any one holds cheap, he'll
Find he cannot live,
　Or die with decent People.
Your business, all, if Old,
　Young, or Children in your Frocks, is

In one short Precept told,
 Which is—" Preserve the Foxes."
  The way to cure all Woe,
   And baffle Fortune's shocks, is
  Singing Tally Ho—
   And " Preserving Foxes."

" Dies sit, aut Nox,"
 Keep constantly repeating,
Man was made to save the Fox,
 And the Hounds were made to eat him.
No care the conscience clogs
 Of one who never mocks his
Duty to the Dogs,
 But lives " Preserving Foxes."
   The way to cure all Woe, &c. &c.

If you this solemn claim
 Should wickedly neglect, you
Will hear the Dogs bark " Shame,"
 And the Puppies won't respect you—
You may in Woe find Mirth,
 In Pillory, or Stocks, Ease,
But you won't find Peace on Earth,
 If you don't " Preserve the Foxes."
   The way to cure all Woe, &c. &c.

Then take care not to swerve,
 And to my Text prove fickle,
For those who won't Preserve,
 We have a Rod in Pickle.
We'll excommunicate,
 For, of all Heterodoxes,

There's no one half so great
  As not "Preserving Foxes."
    The way to cure all Woe, &c. &c.

Ye small Boys, in whose looks
  Learning sees no Lovers,
You may burn your Books,
  If you will keep the Covers;
Let other Histories go,
  Like Gibbon's, Hume's, or Coxe's,
And give all thoughts below
  To "Preserving Fox's."
    The way to cure all Woe, &c. &c.

Of crimes to think 'tis sad,
  Like Burning, Murder, Stealing;
Who does all these is Bad,
  Still, may have Human Feeling.
But He cannot hope to win
  Any sympathy, who knocks his
Head against the Sin
  Of "not Preserving Foxes."
    The way to cure all Woe, &c. &c.

Let the Fox live on your land,
  And We are not unwilling
To let you try your hand
  At any kind of killing:
You may cut up Children, Wives,
  Or shut them up in boxes,
Take, if you please, their lives,
  But oh! "Preserve the Foxes."
    The way to cure all Woe, &c. &c.

And now " Long live the Queen,"
  And may no Foes un-nerve her,
That is, of course we mean,
  If She's a good Preserver.
But the Army, Church, and Crown,
  The Commons, Peers, and Proxies,
Must certainly go down,
  If they don't " Preserve the Foxes."
          The way to cure all Woe,
            And baffle Fortune's shocks, is
          Singing Tally Ho—
            And " Preserving Foxes."

THE COMMISSIONERS.

Tune—JUDY O'CALLAGHAN.

At two o'Clock one day,
  With aspect sad, and frowning,
Some men were seen to stay
  In the charming Street of Downing.
And at the Treasury door,
  That Temple of enjoyment,
Were thus heard to implore
  For a little paid employment.
          " Don't say, Nay,"
            To your poor Petitioners,
          Only pay,
            And make us all Commissioners.

A precious set are we,
   Well worthy your commanding,
Lawyers without a fee,
   And all of six years standing.
The Public seems to know
   How much it will be a gainer,
If off with Reports we go,
   By giving us no Retainer.
       Don't say, Nay, &c. &c.

A Body as well might stay
   Without its Food, or Raiment,
As we face Quarter Day,
   If it does not bring us Payment.
These kind words we beseech,
   To charm our ravished Senses,
" Five Guineas a day to each,
   And his Travelling Expenses."
       Don't say, Nay, &c. &c.

Don't fear that we'll stick fast,
   Ourselves we greatly flatter,
If, so long as payments last,
   We don't find subject Matter.
Wherever we turn our eyes,
   We find Enquiry courted,
And all, beneath the skies,
   Going wrong if not Reported.
       Don't say, Nay, &c. &c.

The Dogs they bark, and bite,
   Engaged in constant quarrels,

Because we do not write
　　Reports upon their Morals.
And even the little Cats,
　　To Hullah's indignation,
Sing Sharp upon the Flats,
　　From want of Investigation.
　　　　　　Don't say, Nay, &c. &c.

Of every thing, small and great,
　　Man, Beast, Bird, Insect, Fish, on
Past, Present, and Future state,
　　Pray, issue a Commission :—
On the Army, Navy, Church,
　　Schools, Rates, Tithes, Taxes, Rental,
On the proper supply of Birch,
　　A Matter fundamental.
　　　　　　Don't say, Nay, &c. &c.

We can dress any Fact,
　　And give it quite a True look,
And soon as it's neatly packed,
　　And served up in a Blue Book.
In style we most succeed,
　　And nothing can be nicer,
For all the world might read,
　　And nobody be the wiser.
　　　　　　Don't say, Nay, &c. &c.

Some people once, 'tis said,
　　For Truth were always striving,
And followed wherever it led ;
　　But this was foolish driving.

In a well-Commissioned mind,
  Such practice merits laughter,
Conclusions, first, we find,
  And Facts to prove them, after.
      Don't say, Nay, &c. &c.

Would you have, what's wrong, look right,
  Our zeal will not get slacker ;
We'll prove that Black is White,
  Or that White is rather Blacker.
So, speak us fair, and smooth,
  Our Terms are worth your Trying,
A Penny a Line for Truth,
  And a Farthing more for Lying.
      Don't say, Nay, &c. &c.

Oh! you sit there in full pride
  Of Treasury Bills, and Dockets,
And let us stand outside,
  To sing with empty Pockets.
But, since you deaf remain
  To us, your Fond Implorers,
To-morrow we'll come again,
  And be your constant Borers.
      Don't say, Nay,
        To your poor Petitioners,
      Only Pay,
        And make us all Commissioners.

THE CHARTISTS.

Tune—YANKEY DOODLE.

———

As all enlightened People see,
    That, now, the only Artists
To make them Happy, Wise, and Free,
    Are thorough-going Chartists,
Pray stop, and listen to my speech,
    You've nothing more to care for,
Except to Bluster, Fight, and Screech,
    Not asking why, or wherefore.
        So, come, my Friends, and all you've got,
          And all you hope for, barter
        For, no one knows exactly what,
          Except, 'tis called " The Charter."

Our Country's struck on Order's Rock,
    Where Sense, and Justice maul it,
So must be taken into Dock,
    That we may over-haul it.
To sheath its Keel, and make it pass
    Unharmed by such a stopper,
The Chartists will find lots of Brass,
    Although they're short of Copper.
        So, come, my friends, and all you've got, &c.

Our Noble minds have quite outgrown
    The need of Schools, or College,
For, when they're greater than our own,
    We'll banish Art, and Knowledge.

For Books there can be no excuse,
    We'll burn all, as we find them,
The only Thoughts we like are loose,
    And who shall dare to bind them.
        So, come, my friends, and all you've got, &c.

We'll make the Army, Law, and Crown,
    Take off each Bit, and Bridle,
We'll turn Precedence upside down,
    And claim the Highest Title
For, far and wide, our Patriot School,
    All Kings and Queens rebuffing,
Declares, " there's no one fit to rule,
    Except a Ragamuffin."
        So, come, my friends, and all you've got, &c.

We'll read the Riot Act to Sense,
    Commanding its dispersion,
Let nothing stay five minutes hence,
    That cannot prove Inversion.
Let Children, doing what they please,
    From Chains Parental slipping,
Make Fathers beg, upon their knees,
    To be excused a Whipping.
        So, come, my friends, and all you've got, &c.

Now, all must quit their former parts
    To spread the Chartists' Praises,
The Gentlemen shall draw in Carts,
    The Horses sit in Chaises.
With Joints, on tyrant Butcher's Hooks,
    We'll fraternise, to free them,
While Legs of Mutton roast the Cooks,
    Or Chickens fricassee them.
        So, come, my friends, and all you've got, &c.

Too long deprived of Nature's Right,
  The mis-named Brute-Creation
Shall, basking in the Charter's Light,
  Enjoy Emancipation.
See Geese, with Patriots allied,
  Exchange a friendly greeting,
Whilst Asses gracefully preside
  At every Public Meeting !!
      So, come, my friends, and all you've got, &c.

The Charter's Points that all may know,
  And prove its good Condition,
We'll forge a Million Names, or so,
  To swell our Grand Petition.
If vile Detractors would disjoint
  It's moral force by prying,
We must stick in another Point,
  The Privilege of Lying.
      So, come, my friends, and all you've got, &c.

And now, that Equal Rights may wreathe
  Our Brows, and burst our Fetters,
We'll keep them down, who are beneath,
  And level all our Betters.
These words we read, and want no more,
  Upon the Charter's Sign-Post,
" Knock all those down, who are before,
  The Devil take the Hindmost."
      So, come, my Friends, and all you've got,
        And all you hope for, barter
      For, no one knows exactly what,
        Except, 'tis called the Charter.

. . . .

Tune—NELLY BLIGH.

———

Says Rowland Hill "the Welsh are Scamps,
    Who ought to be put down,
And have instead of Penny Stamps,
    A Kick worth half a Crown—
For all arrangements have been made
    To give the Fools content,
Their letters may be written, " Paid,"
    And every thing, but—*sent.*
        Letters may—go, or stay,
          Never take it ill,
        But pay, and praise the Clever ways
          Of Mr. Rowland Hill.

And thus facetiously I prove,
    That all they say is stuff,
If they've a Post that will not move,
    Their Post is *fast* enough.
They can write Letters when they choose,
    And, if of Mails bereft,
Their case is like a pair of shoes,
    Just one of ' *Write,* and *Left.*'
        Letters may—go, or stay,
          Never take it ill,
        But pay, and praise the Witty ways
          Of Mr. Rowland Hill!

I really wish to do them good,
    And stop them from being cross,
By showing, how a Christian should
    Endure another's loss,

F

Taught by this thought, let every mind
   Soon find it's care allayed ;
Although their Letters stop behind,
   My Salary is Paid.
      Letters may—go, or stay,
        Never take it ill,
      But pay, and praise the Pious ways
        Of Mr. Rowland Hill!

Since Railways are expensive things,
   Which Letters can't requite,
I'll tie them fast to Pigeon's Wings,
   And hope they may go right :
And if a random shot upset
   My Postmen, as they fly,
Why, some one some-where yet may get
   The Letters in a Pie.
      Letters may—go, or stay,
        Never take it ill,
      But pay, and praise the Curious ways
        Of Mr. Rowland Hill!

And here's a less expensive plan,
   Than Railways, Cars, or Gigs,
I'll send their letters, when I can,
   By any Drove of Pigs:
Who, when they swagger through the streets,
   With bags tied to their tails,
May Grunt to every Pig they meet,
   "We are the Royal Mails!!!"
      Letters may—go, or stay,
        Never take it ill,
      But pay, and praise the 'Sty'-lish ways
        Of Mr. Rowland Hill!

ANSWER OF INDIGNANT WELSHMEN.

Oh! Rowland Hill, if 'tis your will
    To et our griefs remain,
As sure, Sir, as your name is Hill,
    Our speaking will be plain,
For all the good your bounty sheds,
    Our thanks we thus express,
' If you have sold us Penny Heads,
    We'll sell you Your's for less."
        If Letters may—go, or stay,
          We shall take it ill,
      And cannot praise the Head-strong ways
        Of Mr. Rowland Hill!

Don't hope, if quite unable
    To grant what we entreat,
To prove, by any Label,
    Your composition sweet.
For you'll be forced to own a
    Truth, both strange, and new,
Though one Whale swallowed Jonah,
    All W(h)ales can't swallow you.
        Letters may—go, or stay,
          We shall take it ill.
      And cannot praise the Bitter ways
        Of Mr. Rowland Hill!

To Rowland Hill a glass we'll fill,
    And this shall be our toast,
Oh! may a quick delivery still
    Adorn the Penny Post.

To one toast more we'll all agree
　To fill up to the Brim,
" Oh ! may the First Delivery be
　Delivery from Him,"
　　　Then let him go, and if 'tis so,
　　　　We shall not take it ill,
　　　　But laugh, and praise ' the Best of Ways'
　　　　Of Mr. Rowland Hill !

———————

THE BAZAAR.

Tune—LE PETIT TAMBOUR.

————

Walk in, and see the Show,
　Walk in, whoever you are ;
'Tis a Shame, and a Sin, not to come in,
　And see our fine Bazaar.
Here is Peace, without Police,
　And Order kept so well,
That buyers say, as they go away,
　Oh ! what a ' *regular* Sell !'
　　　So, walk in, and see the Show,
　　　　Walk in, who ever you are,
　　　　'Tis a Shame, and a Sin, not to come in,
　　　　And see our fine Bazaar.

Don't fear any Tricks of Trade,
　But buy, without a doubt
That, whatever you choose, you never can use,
　So, it will not soon wear out.

But if your mind's inclined
  To a real want or wish,
Why then, it is clear
  As the sea is near,
That you may go, and Fish.
    So, walk in, and see the Show, &c. &c.

Here are Slippers that fit no foot,
  Gloves that nobody wears,
And Fans that defy fine Ladies, who try
  To give themselves any Airs.
So, stand, with your purse in hand,
  And out your Money pull,
Don't mind, in the least, how much you are fleeced,
  We have plenty of German Wool.
    So, walk in, and see the Show, &c. &c,

Do you seek a Jew, or Greek,
  A Tartar, or a Turk,
Here are specimens placed, to suit each taste,
  In our best Worsted Work.
We can sell, so *au naturel*,
  A Monkey, or an Ass,
That if you buy, you will say, " Oh, I
  Am looking in a Glass."
    So, walk in, and see the Show, &c. &c.

Now a sweet young Lady cries,
  " Indeed, my dear Mama,
" I shall never sleep, if I may may not keep
  " A Stall at this Bazaar.
" For I can so attract each Man,
  " That none will wish to range,
    F 2

" But all agree, when they look at me,
  "Never to ask for change.
      So, walk in, and see the Show, &c. &c.

" Oh! such Charming Goods I'll show,
  " And such a Charming Face,
" That I shall take, and no mistake,
  "All the money in the Place.
" With a glance I'll so entrance,
  " And make all people buy,
" That they need not guess, what brings success,
  " But will know it is ' All, my Eye.' "
      So, walk in, and see the Show,
        Walk in, who ever you are,
      'Tis a Shame, and a Sin, not to come in,
        And see our fine Bazaar.

NATIONAL EDUCATION.

Tune—" A M O, A M A S."

LINGO, *in* THE AGREEABLE SURPRISE.

Sweet visions rise
  Before some Eyes
Of the days, when no such attractions
  For Boys will be
Like the Rule of Three,
  Or Sums in Decimal Fractions.
Of little Urchins
  Begging for Birchings,

From a laudable Emulation,
  To be made to feel
The *warmth* of their zeal
  For NATIONAL EDUCATION.

Now, some very good men,
  (Never mind where, or when,)
Who blessed their lucky stars, in
  Being born in an Age,
When there was such a Rage
  For Prosody, and Parsing,
Said, " A School you must make
  The Clay to bake
Of the Rising Generation,
  (Now coarse, and thick,)
To a *regular brick*,
  By NATIONAL EDUCATION.

Do not be afraid,
  You'll have plenty of aid,
If the design's not shorter
  Than befits the cause,
And our applause,
  So, Hey! for Stone and Mortar.
If you take our advice,
  Don't think about the price.
A Spirit of Calculation
  Quite baffles, and thaws,
True Faith in the cause
  Of NATIONAL EDUCATION.

If you should go too far,
  Fall back on a BAZAAR.

If not, (but 'twould be a pity
   To talk of that yet,)
On whoever you can get
   To serve on the Committee."
Well! the Buildings grow—
   The Cash—not so.
On the Day of Inauguration,
   The good Men run
To see what's done
   For NATIONAL EDUCATION.

I humbly enquire,
   As they all admire,
And say, as they view the Building,
   That the *carving's* very good—
Is it understood--
   That I am to furnish the *gilding*.
" Oh! Sir," cry they,
   " If you mean, ' Who's to pay ?'
We'll pay with a conjugation
   Of the verb ' to Do,'
On purpose for you,
   And NATIONAL EDUCATION.

In an active sense,
   Through each Mood, and Tense
Of that verb we'll readily run, Sir
   Whilst you may rejoice
In the *passive* voice,
   And say ' You're thoroughly done, Sir!'
And as we'll requite
   Your kind invite

To pay, with a *Declination*
  You may quiet your qualms
With Grammatical forms,
  And National Education."

So, these very good Men
  Leave me, there and then,
To soothe, as I may, my senses,
  With the thoughts of their praise,
And of, some of these days,
  Being sued for all the expenses.
Now, the honour is great—
  Still, as I hate
All idle ostentation,
  I am willing, I declare,
To divide my share,
  Of National Education.

On Mr. GLADSTONE *joining the* ABERDEEN
Government in the year 1853.

Tune.—BLACK EYE'D SUSAN.

In Downing Street the Council sat,
    With views as changing as the wind,
An Oxford Don, so sleek and fat,
    Cried "Where shall I our Member find?
" Tell me, you motley Council, tell me true,
    " Can my Sweet William sail with such a crew?"

William, who sat at that High Board,
    Rocked by opinions, to, and fro,
Said "Though I fear I shall be floored,
    Still, nolens, volens, I must go."
Reform, and Jew Bills tumble from his hands,
    And, in a Fix, before his Friend he stands.

"Oh! William, dear, can this be true?
    Some sadly shocking things are said;
Our Faith was anchored fast on you,
    And now we fear you're going a-head.
All Men and Things on Earth will soon be Done,
    If Oxford's Gammoned by her favorite Son.

" Where will that Syllogism be,
    Which seemed once to defy all shocks,
Oxford is William's self, and He
    Is all that should be Orthodox,
How can the splendid inference be firm,
    If you should prove a shifting Middle Term."

Says William, " Hang the Envious race,
 Who tempt with doubts your constant mind,
And say, When men get into Place,
 They leave their Principles behind.
And yet you may believe this, if you will,
 Believe I ought to be your Member still.

" Oh! Oxford—Oxford—Lovely Dear,
 My vows shall ever true remain,
Think not I am what I appear,
 Logic shall make that matter plain,
Dictus simpliciter, though here I be,
 Dictus secundum quid, I'm there with Thee."

The Oxford Don is bothered so,
 His doubts he scarcely can confess ;
But the Clock says that he must go,
 Or be too late for the Express.
He seeks a Cab upon the nearest stand,
 Whilst William from his nose extends his hand.

ON THE REPEAL OF THE ADVERTISEMENT DUTY.

Tune.— . . . .

Worth, Wit, and Beauty,
 Your joy is complete,
The Advertisement Duty,
 Has had a Defeat.
Fiction, and Facts,
 Are free to the Nation,

Without any Tax
   On Imagination.
Now no one need grieve
   At the ills he endures,
If he 'll only believe
   Half he reads of the Cures.
For if any one Dies,
   'Tis for Novelty's sake, or,
That he may patronize
   Some Flash Undertaker.
      Every one cries—Oh! what a Prize,
        Light for the Eyes, and ample Supplies,
      To make us all Healthy, and Wealthy, & Wise,
        Are found in the Magical Word, "Advertise."

First joy of the Day,
   As he wakes from his Nap,
Each Wise man will say,
   Is Mechi's famed Strap;
But if his Beard's rough,
   His pleasure increases,
When blest with that Stuff,
   Called "Patent Euxesis."
For Breakfast, I guess,
   That nothing is finer,
Than Tea bought for less
   Than it's sold for in China.
Whilst Fry to each Taste
   Stands Parentis in Loco,
With his Chocolate Paste,
   And Soluble Cocoa.
      Every one cries, &c.

The Youth, to the Fair
  Who his Passion discloses,
Can't fail if he wear
  A Suit made by Moses.
But if, by some chance,
  The Lady proves fickle,
She's reclaimed by a Glance
  Of a Paletot by Nicoll.
Time can't make his Hair cease,
  But owns its Surpasser,
In "Atkinson's Bear's Grease,"
  Or "Rowland's Macassar,"
Whilst "Truefit's Tinctura,"
  Which makes Black of Yellow,
Must prove quite a Cure for
  The ugliest Fellow.
            Every one cries, &c.

Then if you want Houses,
  The place where to go,
Every Good judge allows, is,
  To Paradise Row :
To see is to learn it—your
  Home must be there,
Beautiful Furniture ;
  Perfect Repair.
Such Views, and Approaches !
  Nor can you till in—know,
What Carts, Cabs, and Coaches,
  You'll see from the window.
I'll stick to my Text—
  Perfection is here,
For a Rent, that is next
  To nothing a year !
            Every one cries, &c.

But if you're Rheumatic,
  Your House you must well stock,
From Cellar to Attic,
  With " Steer's Opodeldoc,"
Such Virtue it deals
  To each part that it touches,
That up fly the Heels,
  And down drop the Crutches.
In Life's last Extremities,
  Send for a Mixture
Of Holloway's Remedies,
  Or Daffy's Elixir,
Such Exquisite Tipple
  Would make an Old Man go,
Or even a Cripple,
  And dance a Fandango.
        Every one cries, &c.

This way, every day,
  The praises ascend
Of those who don't pay,
  But who recommend.
So now, then, before us,
  To fairly decide,
We'll summon a chorus,
  Of those who have tried.
But nothing so strange is,
  As what all the Praise meant ;
Every thing Changes,
  And I'm in amazement.
All's disappointment,
  Every thing wrong goes,

Elixir, and Ointment,
  Coffee, and Congoes.
    Every one cries—Dust for the Eyes,
      Spiders to Catch poor unfortunate Flies,
      Robbery—Jobbery—Gammon, and Lies,
      That's what we mean, when we say, Advertise.

Pray tell me no low Fibs,
  For the whole Stock we hate
Of your cheap Cocoa Nibs,
  And Patent Chocolate.
Let us go, if we must,
  To the Dust without Fuss,
But not first ask the Dust
  To Breakfast with us.
Potion, and Lotion,
  Just make our Limbs worse,
And but help Locomotion
  Of Cash from our Purse.
Every day Holloway
  Somebody kills
Of those, who swallow a
  Box of his Pills.
    Every one cries, &c.

That Villain Moses
  Wickedly flatters ;
To-day's Suit of Clothes
  Is to-morrow's of Tatters :
And, in spite of his Fame,
  We very soon shall know
Of Nicoll's the same,
  And his " Registered Paletot."

The House, that I've got,
　　Decays every minute,
And, unless 'tis the Rot,
　　There is Nothing Dry in it.
There is not a Sound Board,
　　A Shutter, or Shelf,
And, nothing quite floored,
　　Excepting—Myself.
　　　　　Every one cries, &c.

Now, here is my Case,
　　And Buyers may try,
Which wins in the Race,
　　The Truth, or the Lie,
But one thing is plain.—
　　May it give them content,—
The Fact will remain,
　　That their Money is spent.
And here too is one
　　Consolation for wrong,
That, if they are Done,
　　Why so is my Song :
And if not entertained,
　　They have learned the Surprising
Advantage they 've gained,
　　By free Advertising !
　　So, let some one, as wise as a Judge of Assize,
　　　　Settle the case, which leaves me in Surmise,
　　Whether Light for the Eyes,— or Gammon, and Lies,
　　　　Are what we mean, when we say " Advertise."

JOHN BRIGHT.

Tune- " For there's nae luck about the house."

————

Of all odd things, the oddest, I
   Have met with here below,
Is the sad want of Modesty
   In all the Men I know.
I grieve to find how many
   Will think that they are right,
While really there's not any
   One, except myself—John Bright.
      For there's but one Man to Command,
        One Man, who's always right,
      There is but one Man in the Land,
        And that's myself—John Bright.

I don't want even Annual
   Parliaments to meet,
For with my little Manual,
   Your Guidance is Complete.
First let mine, and no other Will,
   In all things be obeyed,
And next—what I think better still,—
   Let no one else be paid.
      For there's but one Man to Command, &c.

Put every Institution down,
   But Bright,—and trust in him,
And do not leave a Single Crown,
   But one with a Broad Brim.

No Church—No State—No Queen—No King—
  No Soldiers to fight,
No Sailors—and no any thing,
  Except Myself—John Bright.
      For there's but one Man to Command, &c.

If Foreign Enemies invade
  With Fifty Thousand Men,
You 'll see them all at once dismayed
  At one Flourish of my Pen.
For I shall write a little Note,
  To make the case so plain,
That every Man will give his Vote
  For Marching back again.
      For there's but one Man to Command, &c.

For I shall merely write, and say,
  Your Venture is unsound,
Th' invasion clearly cannot pay
  Twenty shillings in the Pound.
And the General, quite willing,
  At leave to go will grab,
If I only lend a Shilling
  To help to pay his Cab.
      For there's but one Man to Command, &c.

The Sun is said to rule the Day,
  And the Moon to rule the Night,
But so unevenly—that they
  Should both be ruled by a Bright.
They're quite disorderly, and wrong,
  And very badly taught,
For now, some Days, and Nights are Long,
  And some of them are Short.
      For there's but one Man to Command, &c.

For fair Equality demands
    Them both of equal length,
Just as all Men, throughout all Lands,
    Should be of equal Strength.
All Men (of course excepting One,)
    For Real Power, and Might,
Should be concentrated, and run
    To me alone—John Bright.
        For there's but one Man to Command, &c.

But oh! there's one Perplexity,
    Which much annoys me here,
It is the World's Convexity,
    Because it is a Sphere.
The Land's unlucky Dip, and Seas,
    Put Nations out of Place,
And stop the poor Antipodes
    From looking at my Face.
        For there's but one Man to Command, &c.

To make it clear to all Men's Eyes,
    That, what's beneath my Hat,
Holds every thing that's Good, and Wise,
    The World must first be flat.
And very, very flat indeed,
    I fear the World must be,
Before I perfectly succeed
    To make it trust in Me.
        For there's but one Man to Command,
          One Man that's always right;
        There is but one Man in the Land,
          And that's myself—John Bright.

APPENDIX.

SONGS NOT PREVIOUSLY PRINTED.

. . . .

On the Presentation of (before the means of Payment were provided) a Park to the People of Birmingham.

Tune—THE YOUNG MAN FROM THE COUNTRY, WHO KEPT COMPANY WITH ME.

I sing a Song of Birmingham, of Pockets ill supplied,
Performance very narrow, and Promise very wide.
To make all clear to every ear, I beg you'll hear the Prayer,
That bears the Mark of the Town Clerk, Town Councillors,
    and Mayor.
  So Pity, pray, poor Patriots, perversely pressed to pay.

For some relief to cure our grief, our claims we strongly urge,
The Councillors of Birmingham, and Mayor Mr. Sturge.
A patriot set, who now are met, to fret at being taught,
That even they may have to pay, sometimes for what they've
    bought,
  So Pity, pray, poor Patriots, perversely pressed to pay.

For this would shake, and no mistake, the credit and renown,
For Counterfeits and clever cheats, of our ingenious Town.
When Brass by strange and sudden change, a Gilded face has
    got,
And all is allegorical, and stands for what it's Not,
  So Pity, pray, poor Patriots, perversely pressed to pay.

That Virtue too may have its Due, and treatment just the
    same,
When not enough of Real Stuff, we always use the Name.
And since none Praise expensive ways, a Novel stock we
    keep,
Of Patent Liberality, that is extremely cheap.
  So Pity, pray, poor Patriots, perversely pressed to pay.

What more complete and neat Receipt, to strew Life's Path
    with Flowers,
Was ever known than "Hold our Own," and "Give what is not
    ours."
Who follows us, without the fuss of giving gains the sense,
And a Man's a good Samaritan, without the Oil and Pence.
  So Pity, pray, poor Patriots, perversely pressed to pay.

That this good Rule should neither cool or slumber in the
    dark,
To elevate its Social state, we gave our Town a Park,
With ample ground, for safe and sound we thought was the
    advice,
That as our Way was not to pay, we need not mind the Price.
  So Pity, pray, poor Patriots, perversely pressed to pay.

That fresh Delight might crown the sight, we asked our Gra-
    cious Queen,
To what some Few may call a *Do*, but we, a Glorious Scene.
And all things went to our Content, until that Dismal Day,
When we were pressed, and much distressed by a Request to
    pay.
  So Pity, pray, poor Patriots, perversely pressed to pay.

In that short Sound what Grief was found, we Buyers scarce
    can tell,
We wish the word seemed as absurd to those who had to sell.
And we 're afraid the Gift we've made, some have misunder-
    stood,
And Blind to our Grand Presents, find our absence just as
    good.
    So Pity, pray, poor Patriots, perversely pressed to pay.

Now to compose and end our Woes, we modestly must ask,
That you, your fair and proper Share, will take up our Task.
Let us the Pains and all the Gains of Benefaction win,
And you the Joy without alloy, of furnishing the Tin,
    So Pity, pray, poor Patriots, perversely pressed to pay.

Let there and then, all Honest Men their Duty not forget,
But open wide, with proper pride, their Purse to pay our Debt.
And own though short of Tin we're thought, that nothing can
    surpass,
Great Birmingham, for serving them, with good supplies of
    Brass.
    So Pity, pray, poor Patriots, perversely pressed to pay.

RAILWAY SONG.

Tune—. . . . .

———

How happy to live in these fast going times !
And find compensation for sorrow and crimes ;
A Plaster for Loss, and a cure for Disgrace
In the simple Prescription of Plenty of Pace ;
Though Fortune, her Wheel, may reverse with a Frown,
She is equally pleased, with an Up or a Down,
When each with a rival attraction assails,
In getting up Steam, or in laying down Rails.
  So we cut all progression by Horses and Sails,
  And turn up our Noses at Stages and Mails,
  For the Doctors prescribe for each ill that assails,
  No Remedy like Locomotion by Rails.

They first call a Meeting, then spend a whole week,
In preparing Impromptus for movers to speak,
Whose bright Resolutions completely outshine
The Skill of the Poet in gilding a *Line*.
And in Pious alarm of our failing to scan
With Optics unclouded their exquisite plan,
And of taking its Manifold wonders on Trust,
Their very first summons is Down with the Dust.
  So we cut all progression by Horses and Sails, &c.

I listen with Wonder, and hear with Delight,
That whatever was wrong is put suddenly right,
And find myself blest with an ample supply,
Of all that I want—but the Money to buy.

If that should be short, my Encouragers say,
That the Profits have merely mistaken their way,
And taken another, but little the worse,
That is called *their* Prospectus instead of *my* Purse.
    So we cut all progression by Horses and Sails, &c.

Now look at the Flag of Improvement unfurled,
And the Barter of knowledge all over the World,
In a Moment, the Ladies of China express,
To those at the Pole their Ideas of Dress.
With the speed of the Lightning, kind Messages pass,
If I send to a Friend to declare he's an ass,
I am favoured before Recollection is cool,
With an answer to tell me, that I am a Fool.
    So we cut all progression by Horses and Sails, &c.

Poor Cupid is forced, though the Slaves of his yoke
Submit as of old to Hot Water and Smoke,
To a change which his Passion for Symmetry stings,
And to wear a great Chimney instead of his wings.
The Lover in aid of his Gentle Pursuit,
Now takes a Steam Whistle instead of his Lute,
And sparing his sighs, if the Lady rebuff,
Sends off as his Proxy an Engine to puff.
    So we cut all progression by Horses and Sails, &c.

If I with Directors attempt to dispute,
At their Demonstration objection is mute,
My Dread of a Mountain they treat with Disdain,
By showing this Method of making it *Plain*.
For they tell me—" Come with us and trust in our Skill,
Of getting a rise out of you, and the Hill ;
Only take a few Shares, and you'll find after that,
That wherever you are—there's a *Regular Flat*."
    So we cut all progression by Horses and Sails, &c.

And now in one Toast all our Blessings to sum,
Here's the Money that's gone, and the Railway to come!
If your Eyes are too Dull to behold it as True,
Put Spurs to your Fancy, and ride for the view.
On arches above—and through Tunnels below,
Through air, and through earth, see it merrily go,
Enriching our Land, and improving our Trade,
With only one fault—that it has not been made.
　　So we cut all progression by Horses and Sails,
　　And turn up our Noses at Stages and Mails,
　　For the Doctors prescribe for each ill that assails,
　　No Remedy like Locomotion by Rails.

RAILWAY SONG.

Tune.

WILL YOU COME TO THE BOWER I HAVE SHADED FOR YOU.

Will you come to the Bower I have shaded for you,
The attraction is old—I must get something New.
Then come to my Railroad, and when you are there,
You will find yourself in—a more *Shady* affair.
　　Will you, Will you, Will you, Will you, take a few Shares,
　　Will you, Will you, Will you, Will you, take a few Shares.

Oh! come to the Railroad I've sketched out for you,
It's a capital Thing—quite certain to do.
Quite certain to do—those who are not afraid,
But whose Names are all booked, and whose money is all paid.
　　Will you, Will you, Will you, Will you, take a few Shares, &c.

If you wish to know what terminus, and traffic we have got,
Oh! we have a splendid traffic in—nobody knows what.
And our Terminus it gives me Pride and Pleasure to declare,
Is at that fast Improving place, called—Nobody knows where.
  Will you, Will you, Will you, Will you, take a few Shares, &c.

The Prettiest of Pretty games, which any one can choose,
Is surely that where all must win, and Nobody can lose.
Come play then at my Railroad, where, so Projectors say,
Every Person must receive, whilst No one has to pay.
  Will you, Will you, Will you, Will you, take a few Shares, &c.

For a Railroad is a Reservoir, without a Leak, or Spout,
Where every thing keeps running in—whilst Nothing can come
        out,
Where Nothing can come out—and to prove it, I'll begin,
By asking many People who have put there Money in,
  Will you, Will you, Will you, Will you, take a few Shares, &c.

So whilst the Blessed Bulls and Bears stand round us in a
        Ring,
In honour of our Railroad, a Duet we will sing.
The Part of Rook, I'll keep myself, for you might think it Dull,
But you'll find the Part quite suitable, that's written for the
        Gull.
  Will you, Will you, Will you, Will you, take a few Shares.
  Will you, Will you, Will you, Will you, take a few Shares.

INDEX.

APPENDIX.

www.ingramcontent.com/pod-product-compliance
Lightning Source LLC
Chambersburg PA
CBHW021416090426

42742CB00009B/1159